BREAKING COVENANTS WITH COUNTERFEITS

Journey to Freedom—A Love Story

EREKA N. THOMAS
FOREWORD BY DR. EBONI L. TRUSS

Cocoon to Wings
PUBLISHING

Printed in the United States of America
ISBN: 978-1-963964-07-3 (Paperback)
ISBN: 978-1-963964-08-0 (Digital Online)

Library of Congress Control Number: 2024938477

Published by Cocoon to Wings Publishing
7810 Gall Blvd., #311
Zephyrhills, FL 33541
www.CocoontoWingsBooks.com
(813) 906-WING (9464)

Scriptures marked AMP are taken from the HOLY BIBLE, AMPLIFIED BIBLE Copyright © 2015 by The Lockman Foundation, La Habra, CA 90631. All rights reserved.

Cover Design by ETP Creative

BREAKING COVENANTS WITH COUNTERFEITS

Journey to Freedom—A Love Story

CONTENTS

Acknowledgments .... *vii*

Foreword .... *ix*

Preface .... *xiii*

Introduction .... *xvii*

CHAPTER 1   **THE SET UP**   1

CHAPTER 2   **THE EXCHANGE**   11

CHAPTER 3   **THE TRUTH**   23

CHAPTER 4   **DELIVERANCE**   37

CHAPTER 5   **THE AUTHENTICITY ADVANTAGE**   47

CHAPTER 6   **REDEMPTION**   65

CHAPTER 7   **FREEDOM STRATEGY**   77

Bibliography 81

ACKNOWLEDGMENTS

This book would never have seen the light of day had it not been for the continuous prompting of the Holy Spirit to push through, the love of Father God to sustain me, and the sacrifice of Jesus as the example of looking at the blessing for someone else before me to motivate me to keep moving forward.

I would like to thank my family for being my stability through this process and holding down the fort. For loving me through my process and giving me the space and freedom to evolve. My publisher, sister-friend, and BB (Business Bae), Stephanie Outten, for always supporting me, laughing with me, encouraging me, covering me in prayer, and not allowing me to give up. I have to thank my mentor and friend, Dr. Eboni L. Truss. Thank you for being the Ananias to my Paul.

To all my family, friends, church members, co-workers, mentors, coaches, etc., you have helped me in ways words can't describe. Thank you for the kind words, the questions, the inspiration, the long talks, the prayers, the shoulders to lean on, and all the ways that you have helped to shape this journey. I love you all dearly.

FOREWORD

It's an honor to be asked to write the foreword for a book that promises such a profound journey to authenticity and transformation. Ereka's story is not just a narrative; it's a beacon of hope for all those who have ever felt trapped in the maze of others' expectations.

From the very first page, she invites you into the depths of her experiences, sharing the raw emotions and struggles that have shaped her journey. And in doing so, she offers a roadmap for liberation—a testament to the transformative power of God toward self-love and authenticity.

Throughout Breaking Covenants with Counterfeits, Ereka weaves together the threads of her experiences with grace and eloquence. Her words resonate with authenticity, reminding us all that true freedom lies not in conformity, but in wholeheartedly embracing who God has called us to BE. As you accompany her on her journey, you too will be inspired to embark on your own journey of self-discovery, armed with the knowledge that you are worthy of your Father's love and acceptance.

One of the most remarkable aspects of this book is Ereka's descriptions of how she was able to navigate the complexities of relationships and identity. With honesty and insight, she explores the impact of societal pressures on our sense of self-worth, and the profound healing that comes from breaking free from toxic patterns and embracing healthy, authentic connections. Her willingness to share the highs and lows of her personal relationships is a testament to her courage and vulnerability; you will find solace and inspiration through the experiences she shares with you.

But perhaps the most powerful message of Breaking Covenants with Counterfeits is the reminder that this is a journey — a journey that requires courage, resilience, and partnership with God – IF your goal is to break free from the constraints of the past, and to embrace a future filled with love, joy, and limitless possibility. Her courage, vulnerability, and unwavering commitment to authenticity serve as a powerful reminder that true freedom begins when we dare to agree with God and embrace every aspect of who we are.

Words do not adequately express how honored I am to call Ereka my mentee, my friend, and my sister. Her story has had a profound impact on me personally. It was quite literally a conversation with her that prevented me from making a "covenant with a counterfeit" myself. I have no doubt that you and others around the world will be similarly inspired by her journey, and I am honored to play a small part in sharing this - her love letter of freedom - to you.

So to you, the one who has chosen to embark on this journey with Ereka N. Thomas, "Freedom Facilitator," I say this: may you be inspired by her courage, uplifted by her vulnerability, and empowered to embrace the fullness of who you are.

Your heart is prepared. Your mind is open. And you deserve to be FREE!

Dr. Eboni L. Truss
Founder of the Un-Becoming Movement
www.EboniLTruss.com

PREFACE

I was sitting at a diner across from my mentor, Dr. Eboni L. Truss, Founder of the Un-Becoming movement (yourunbecoming.com). She had come to town to spend time with her mentor. I caught wind of Dr. Eboni's visit on Facebook when I saw her post about it. I'd gone to college with her mentor and reached out to her to ask if they had any breaks in their schedule so I could drive down and say hello. We decided that I would take Dr. Eboni back to the airport so she and I could have breakfast before then since she had to check out of her Airbnb much earlier than her flight. On the drive over, I was thinking of how to bring up the topic of wanting to hear more about her weight loss journey, which she previously shared during a virtual session she was facilitating, which I had been late to. I overheard her as she was finishing a conversation with one of her mentees and found out she had lost over 100 pounds. My weight was one of those continuous battles that I'd fought most of my life, and I couldn't resist the opportunity to pick her brain about it. I'd almost forgotten to ask once we sat down to eat, but it triggered my memory after she ordered her food. She was on a keto diet, and I'd vaguely heard some things, but I was thinking to myself, *I could eat like that.*

"I really wanted to talk to you about keto and your weight loss journey," I said as we waited for our food.

"Before we do that, I want to ask you, 'Why did you renounce your sorority membership?" she stared at me, waiting for an answer.

I had this *come again* look on my face as to say *can you repeat that,* because it seemed like it came out of left field. I couldn't understand why that would even be of interest to her. My sorority affiliation and my renouncing it seemed like another life compared to where I was and a foreign topic to the people I was then keeping company with. I considered the woman before me a powerful, strong, confident woman of God who had a real relationship with God. She was the founder of the Un-Becoming movement, which was how we connected in the first place. Un-becoming was the revelation that she received from God about how we spend our whole lives trying to become something or someone when, in fact, God created us from the foundation of the world with an original intent. The process of un-becoming is to get to that place of be-ing who He created us to be. I didn't understand why my renouncing the sorority would even matter to her, so I asked why she was interested in knowing. She said she would tell me after I told her why I renounced.

Earlier that morning, when I'd arrived at the Airbnb, Dr. Eboni's mentor was waiting at the door, and when I walked in, she introduced me and Dr. Eboni as if she thought we were strangers. In her introduction, she said, "...and Ereka is a member of (organization name intentionally omitted) sorority." I corrected her and said I was no longer a member, which prompted an "Oh, that's right" from her as she casually went on from there. I was somewhat confused because she and I reconnected a couple of months back to catch up on life since college. During our conversation, we talked in depth about me no longer being a member of the sorority. I brushed it off until the topic came up again at breakfast.

I recounted my entire story to Dr. Eboni from the beginning until the point where God showed me that my sorority affiliation was not His will for my life and that I had made a covenant that had to be broken. How, ultimately, I exchanged my true identity for a counterfeit. Telling that story was not something I did often. I saw it as a part of my past that didn't really have any relevance in the life that I was currently living. After sharing, I told her, "Now tell me why you wanted to know." She told me her story and how that moment was a divine intervention. She had come to Florida with some specific questions for God; essentially, it was a line-in-the-sand moment for her. She shared how, at different times in her past, opportunities came up for her that never seemed to work out and how my story gave her clarity that it was God protecting her.

I was in a state of shock, like a mouth-opened kind of shock. I had no clue that something I shared about my life, which by that point was a regular everyday life, could make a difference in someone else's life. They say hindsight is 20/20, but I realize that moment was a turning point for me. I had no idea what I was about to walk into and what God was about to do in my life, but He had my yes.

This book is about my story, and it is just that—my story. My prayer is that through my transparency and vulnerability, you can peg yourself and uncover the counterfeits in your life. That you will subsequently make a decision to partner with God on your own journey to be free to be all He created you to be… authentically.

INTRODUCTION

You are probably wondering what "breaking covenants with counterfeits" even means. I promise you; I did not come up with the title in hopes of getting your attention. Breaking covenants with counterfeits is a real thing. Let me provide you with a definition to give you a better understanding of what all this actually means. According to Webster's Dictionary, A counterfeit is something "made in the exact imitation of something valuable or important with the intention to deceive or defraud" (Merriam-Webster, n.d.). For example, a cubic zirconia was made to look exactly like a diamond but is far less unique and valuable. At first glance, you can't really tell the difference, but a closer look reveals the truth. A covenant "is a binding agreement or a contract between two parties" (Merriam-Webster, n.d.). I can already see the wheels turning in your head. You are probably thinking, *If a covenant is a binding agreement between two parties and a counterfeit is something that was created to imitate with the intent to deceive, why would anyone make a covenant with a counterfeit?* I don't believe we do it intentionally yet; unknowingly, we do it all the time.

I believe every time we exchange the truth for a lie; we make a covenant with a counterfeit. *That's a strong statement, Ereka!* you might say. It is a strong statement. For example, according to Psalms 139, when God says that we are fearfully and wonderfully made, and we say, "I'm too this" or "I'm not enough that," we exchange His truth for a lie. We come into agreement with the lie. We, in fact, make a covenant with a counterfeit. You need me to explain it a little more, right? Well, let's take a baby who comes into this world. The Word of God says that He knew us in the womb. He formed us. (Jeremiah 1:5) So when we get here on earth, the very destiny that God created us for is stitched into our DNA. However, as the child matures, they hear, see, and experience things that start forming what they believe about themselves. This takes the child on a journey to discover who they are and what they want to do with their life. They look externally for the answer. They find what seems to be "it," a career, a relationship, acceptance, or confidence. But what seems to be "it" soon reveals that it is not *it* at all.

Think about that relationship you thought was "it." He or she was "the one" only to find out otherwise. Or that career path that promised prosperity and prestige, but you had no peace. I once heard that when you don't know the purpose of a thing, you will abuse or misuse it. I think that applies to our very lives. Who knows the purpose of a thing except the creator? Our Creator knows precisely who and why He created us to be. Our job is to find out who that is through our relationship with Him. God did not create us to experience life without Him but in partnership with Him.

It all seems so simple, doesn't it? The problem is not that we don't desire God's best, His original intent. We all do. However, it's not about what we desire but what we believe. What do we believe about ourselves, God, and His purpose for our lives? It reminds me of Abraham in the Bible. He was promised a child with his wife, Sarah. They started getting older, and the promise was getting harder and harder to hold on to. They decided to take matters into their own hands and birthed a counterfeit. Ishmael was a son, but he was not the promise. Eventually, Abraham and Sarah did receive the promised son, Issac. History shows a constant war between the descendants of the promised son and the counterfeit. I wonder if that would have been the case if they believed God without wavering from the promise.

In this book, I intend to show you through my personal journey how we can be set up to believe a lie about who we are and subsequently make an exchange for what we think we lack. I spent most of my life trying to be what I considered "normal," but ended up living an abnormal life - a counterfeit. I wasn't trying to discover who God created me to be. What I was trying to do was to become who I thought I should be. This idea of *normal*.

My mentor, Dr. Eboni, taught me the "first-word principle." She said the first word you hear when you ask God a question is God. The next is you, with your analytical self, questioning whether it's you or God, and the third is the devil saying, "Now you know that wasn't God!" We hear God. Point blank, period.

One of her mentors and friends, Dubb Alexander, Founder of School of Kingdom, says, "We are one with the One who knows all the things, and He loves to talk to you." It's personal. Your personal God desires for you to be free to be all He created you to be. Living a life from a place of being authentically you starts with clearing the foundation and stripping away every false thing or counterfeit that is not in alignment with who God created you to be. There are advantages when the real you is revealed, the authentic you.

Throughout this book, I have included some time of reflection for you to journal with the Lord. To ask the questions to help you identify areas in your own life that just don't seem quite right, but you couldn't put your finger on it. Allow God, Jesus, and Holy Spirit to take you on a journey of discovery to break covenants with counterfeits and unlock the advantages of being authentically you.

CHAPTER 1

THE SET UP

One day, I was at my grandmother's house and found a picture of myself. I had to be about five years old. I wore a blue tank top with yellow trim, white shorts with red trim (I don't think my clothes ever matched as a child), and my grandmother's shoulder-length wig and knee-high patent leather boots. I used to love playing "dress-up" in my grandmother's clothes when she'd take them off after getting home from work. They always smelled of Budweiser® and White Diamonds from the two tall Budweiser beers she would drink after work and the Liz Claiborne White Diamonds perfume she wore. I remembered the day that picture was taken. I was in the living room dancing and putting on a show for my aunts and their friends when my grandmother walked through the door from work. I told everyone I was entertaining to wait so I could put on my "costume." I ran to my grandmother's room and grabbed her wig and boots, but I couldn't find her shirt that I would wear as a dress. Time was wasting, and my "fans" were waiting, so the end result was what was captured in the picture. I stared at the photo in my hand and felt a little sad. I remembered the feeling that little girl had at that moment. She loved to dance, was always the center of attention, and would talk your ear off. However, the person staring at the picture was petrified of even the thought of being the center of attention, afraid to speak up for fear of rejection, and left the dance moves behind closed doors. So how did the spicy and free little girl turn into the complete opposite? To answer that question, we have to start at the genesis.

The Genesis

My mom had me when she was 17 years old. My dad was 21, but he was in and out of jail. My mom and I lived with my grandparents and my aunts and uncles. I was treated more like the baby of the family since my parents were so young. So, my aunts and uncles were like older siblings. I was told I was spoiled. My uncle tells a story to this day of how he would take me to school with him, and everybody wanted to hold me. Then, he would have to get on the loudspeaker in the front office and ask whoever had me to return me to the office. I honestly don't remember being told no. I literally had whatever I wanted when I wanted it. That especially included food. My grandmother had me eating mashed-up collard greens and cornbread at three months old. Wherever I went, I was fed. My dad's brother used to babysit me after my dad picked me up from daycare. He would take me to this place down the hill from his house, and I would sit on this particular stool, and these nice ladies would feed me peanuts and candy. It wasn't until I became an adult that I learned the place was a pool hall and the nice ladies were prostitutes. As I said, my parents were young. LOL. Even though I was active and loved to play outside, I didn't really grow much in height, but I grew a whole lot in width. One of my neighbors joked about it one day when I was outside playing and said, "You ain't getting no taller, but you sure are getting wider."

Eventually, my mom and I moved in with my dad after he got settled. He had a small, two-bedroom apartment across the street from a lake. I guess you could say things started to change after that. It had been me and my mom up until that point. At my grandparent's house, me and my mom slept in the same bed, and when she wasn't around, my aunts and uncles looked after me. When we moved in with my dad, I was forced to sleep in my own room all by myself. I started out sleeping between my mom and dad, but one night, I said I didn't like him sleeping with us because he made me hot with his body heat, and that was the last night I slept with them. I was told I cried all night, but I don't remember much about that night. It wasn't long after that my sister came, and eventually, she would sleep on the twin bed next to me. That's all I really wanted: a sister to sit next to me in the back seat of the car. My brother came two years later. I didn't ask for him, though (insert side-eye emoji). Just like that, I went from being the baby to the oldest. There were expectations about who I was supposed to be and how I was supposed to act. My father was extremely critical. If it wasn't his way, it was wrong. There are three ways that I learned you can respond to criticism. You can fight against it, you can run away from it, or you can conform to it. I chose the latter. I chose to be a people pleaser. My father didn't just criticize. Back then, he was loud and cursed a lot. He threw out F-bombs like they were conjunctions in a sentence. Every word of criticism came with scolding. I tried my best to do it "right the first time" to avoid the yelling. Don't get me wrong; I knew my father loved me. However, his method of communication, coupled with the constant correction, had my young self walking on eggshells. I started to conform to what he considered "right." I learned to color in his lines. He would jokingly say I had a "cow mouth" and would imitate how loud I was when I talked. I translated that as a problem to fix, so I learned to be quiet. He talked about my weight constantly. What that translated to me was being "fat" was "wrong." I didn't know how to fix that "problem," so I learned how to hide. I tried to blend in with the background as much as possible. What I learned became what I believed to be true about myself and about how everyone else viewed me. I always feared getting "it" wrong; I feared the rejection. I feared the correction and tried to avoid it as much as possible.

What you talkin''bout, Willis?

It was right around the time I turned seven or eight that my grandmother would have these family gatherings where her cousins would come to visit from out of town. During one of those gatherings, my Aunt Freddie (who was actually my grandmother's cousin, but we called her "Aunt") grabbed me and hugged me real tight with her super long fingernails that always had me wondering how she used the bathroom, said, "Where is that little girl that used to talk us half to death?" My eyes widened with a "What you talkin' 'bout, Willis?" look on my face, an ode to the 70's sitcom *Different Strokes*. I had no clue who she was referring to. I didn't think she was talking about me. Not me! I was shy. I was quiet. I was fat. That was who I was. It didn't hurt that those were words others used to describe me. At that time, I hated going to my grandma's house when she had company. I hated the thought of people looking at me. I did everything I could to draw attention away from myself. I felt like all eyes were on me, looking with disapproval.

I hated the person I had become. Being "fat" made me different, and no matter how I tried to camouflage it by wearing oversized dark clothes, I still stood out, which made me a target for bullying. In grade school, I hated going shopping for school clothes. I felt like every eye was on me, thinking, *what is the "fat" girl going to find to fit her?* There were no stores that sold large sizes for young people. You dressed like either an old lady or a child. Sears was the ONLY store that sold plus-sized clothes for kids. Back then, they called them "Pretty Plus" for girls and "Husky" for boys. Nowadays, with all the body positivity messages, you can find extended sizes in almost anything made. With all the added hormones and genetically modified organisms (GMOs) in foods these days, almost everybody could be "pretty plus."

When I was growing up, though, not so much. It seemed like everywhere I turned; I was reminded of my size. I tried going into a store once that catered to "juniors." As soon as I walked in, the store clerk quickly let me know that they didn't carry my size there. I would give my mother the blues when we would go school shopping. I always had an attitude because I felt like people were watching us. This one time, the local news station was taping a back-to-school segment at the mall, and I ran, trying to hide behind columns or anything else that would keep me out of view. When I got home and turned on the TV that night, there I was on the news, ducking from the camera.

My mom signed us up for Weight Watchers. This was the first time we would try and "do something" about my weight. At the first group meeting, I was so embarrassed. I was the only child in a room full of adults, and they asked me how my week went. I almost passed out. It all reinforced the fact that I was "different." I didn't want to do anything different than what my peers were doing. I didn't want to think about my weight or dieting or any of that. I just wanted to blend in and be "normal."

I was a pretty smart kid in school, but I learned that being "too" smart made you a nerd, which was just another thing to get bullied about. I decided to fly below the radar. Smarter than the "regular" kids, I didn't have to be in classes with them and risk getting bullied, but not too smart to be considered a nerd.

Once I got to sixth grade, I started feeling slightly more "comfortable" in my own skin. Sixth grade was the upper echelon of grade school. I had friends. I was even considered "cool." I wasn't being bullied anymore. One day, I came to school wearing a "fresh" outfit. Neon or loud colors, as we called them, were in and I had on hot pink everything. Hot pink sweatshirt, hot pink and white pinstriped pants, and a hot pink Madonna bow in my hair to top it off. I looked like I just got off the set of a Cindy Lauper "Girls Just Wanna Have Fun" video shoot. I knew I looked good, and for the first time in a long time, I was okay with being seen. I was literally the talk of the school. That was a great day.

Once I got to junior high school, I went back into my shell. I started getting bigger. When I was in elementary school, I would spend the summers at a summer day camp. Once I stopped, I spent the summers watching soap operas and eating, so every year, I went up a size. I was embarrassed about my body, so I wore oversized clothes to hide my shape.

I hated being me so much that I started to fantasize about being someone else. I would live out my day going through the motions but replay it in my head as someone else. In my fantasy world, the coolest girl in school was my cousin, and the finest boy was my boyfriend. I imagined how I looked, how I dressed, and even the things I would say. I got so good at pretending to be someone else that, even in my dreams, I was this fantasy person.

Funny enough, at home with my immediate family, I was the life of the party. I was always making jokes (my entire family is hilarious, by the way), and as I mentioned before, I loved to dance. I could out-dance anyone in my family or friend group. I assumed I got my dance skills from my grandmother because my mother has NO rhythm. I always wanted to be in the band at school and dance during half-time at the football games, but the thought of people seeing me in a band uniform was a firm "not gonna happen." It wasn't like there weren't other "big" people in the band, but I thought maybe they didn't care what people thought about them, and that wasn't me.

Physical Education (PE) was the worst class ever invented. You had to "dress-out" or change into these little bitty shorts and a t-shirt in front of everyone and then participate in physical activity. Well, I was short and had stubby legs. So, during a kickball game, everyone kept kicking the ball toward me because I wasn't fast enough to get to the ball. This one girl on my team said, "If you miss one more ball, I'ma kick yo fat ass!" That was the last day I "dressed out." As an added bonus, I was told that you didn't have to attend summer school if you failed PE. I got all As, Bs, and an F that semester.

Unbeknownst to me, the enemy's plan for my life was playing out nicely. My value and my self-worth were wrapped up in what I felt other people thought of me. As sad as it may seem, other people's opinions, family or foe, would define my life for many years to come.

THE EXCHANGE

O ne day in high school, I went over to a friend's house, and we were looking through some pictures in her photo album. One picture stood out.

"Who is that?" I asked. "She looks familiar."

"Oh, that's my neighbor. She went away to college last year," she said.

I remember seeing this girl in school; she reminded me a lot of myself. Shy, quiet, always looking down. That wasn't how she looked in this photo, though. She was standing in front of what must have been her house, dressed in bright Cross Colours (a Hip-hop clothing brand from the '90s) shorts with a matching "Forever My Lady" Jodeci (a 90s R&B group) jacket holding a walking cane decorated in the same colors. She had

11

this big smile on her face, and even though it was just a picture, she didn't look shy and quiet anymore. She looked bold, confident, and sure of herself. There were some funny-looking letters on her jacket, so I asked my friend, "What are those?"

"Oh, those are her sorority letters," she said matter-of-factly.

S-o-r-o-r-i-t-y, I visualized the way it was spelled in my mind. I wanted to make sure I memorized it to recall it later. I had never heard of a sorority before, but I subconsciously concluded that one could leave home to go off to college and come back a new person by joining a sorority. I spent the remainder of high school focusing on doing whatever I needed to get to college.

That fall, I went away to college. The University of South Florida (USF) was not my first choice. I was all set to attend the University of Florida (UF) in Gaines-ville, Florida, on a four-year scholarship. I was preparing to pay for housing when my future roommate said she got accepted to her first choice and would no longer attend UF. There was no way I was going to school without knowing anyone, so I hopped on the USF bandwagon, where a couple of my other friends would be attending. My mom was scrambling to help me get accepted before the deadline. I got in, and the stage was set.

Since I had two friends attending school with me, I had to choose one to be my roommate. I chose the one who I could be more of myself around. Trying to pretend to be someone you are not, is exhausting. My college crew consisted of myself, my roommate, her summer roommate, and her roommate's best friend. It was the four of us. All the time. Everywhere. This one basketball player nicknamed us "The Get-Along-Gang" after the children's show in the early '90s and eventually renamed us "The Cutie Pie Posse." We had a theme song and everything. Shoutout to the Cutie Pie Posse! My crew was cute, and even though I felt like the sidekick, I was just happy to be in the number. My mom was so afraid that I was hanging with skinny girls because she said that skinny friends would break your heart. In my experience, it was the fat friends who were always competing with you that caused me grief. I liked my crew just how we were. We were all unique. I didn't have to compete with them, and they accepted me for me.

Eyes On the Prize

During orientation week, they had a welcome party for the freshmen. It was my first college party, and it was packed. The DJ was spinning the hottest jams. It was like nothing I had ever seen. I had only been to a couple of parties in high school, and they were nothing like this. I quickly made my way to the wall. Even though my insides were screaming, *get out there on the dance floor and show them what you got*, the voice in my head told me that all eyes would be on me and to lay low. So, I stayed in that one spot the entire night, bobbing my head. Every now and then, one of the posse members would come over and check on me. I was chillin' on the wall observing everyone and secretly studying the latest dance moves so I could try them when I got back to the privacy of my own home with my family. The room parted like the Red Sea when the DJ played a popular song. These girls were in a line doing a dance but moving forward simultaneously, like a train or a stroll, as I learned they were called. It was like the step show moves I had seen earlier in the week at one of the Greek step shows, the coordinated routines performed by African American Greek letter fraternities and sororities, but this was different. They were on beat with the music, and their moves were amazing and like a synchronized dance. I was mesmerized. The way the crowd moved out of the way for them let me know they demanded respect. I could see that some of them were wearing sorority paraphernalia, but theirs were different colors than the girl I saw in the picture back in high school. These girls were stomping as hard as dudes but still lady-like. That was it. If I were going to be in a sorority, I wanted to be in that one.

Even though I loved the idea of going to parties, I stayed in my room on Friday and Saturday nights the entire first semester. I secretly hoped that someone would insist that I come with them because I was too afraid to ask if I could tag along. I don't remember precisely how it happened, but by my second semester, I was attending the parties and hugging the walls. One of the Cutie Pie Posse members started "hanging out" with this guy who was a great dancer. He and his brother would dress like twins and get out on the floor for a mini show during the parties. When Michael Jackson's *Remember the Time* video came out, there was a dance break scene that became the hottest dance move. I don't know what it was called, but we called it the "Michael Jackson." One day, the guy broke out in the dance at a party and motioned for the Posse and me to join him and his brother. They pulled me out there, and for a few seconds, I forgot about who was watching me and what they were thinking about me and did my thing. So much so that some people wanted me to show them how to do it afterward. I still hugged the wall during parties, but by then, I had one song that made me get out on the floor and dance. My favorite time at the parties, though, was watching the sororities and fraternities stroll. The thing about it was sorority members came in all shapes, sizes, and colors, and no matter what, they all looked confident, proud, and bold. I wanted that. I needed that.

Planting the Seed

A couple of years later, the Resident Assistant (RA) on the floor of my college dorm was a member of the sorority that I was interested in. Her sorority was having a "study hall," and I asked my RA what time it started just to confirm. She told me the time and asked if I was "interested." Meaning if I was interested in "pledging" her sorority. In African American Greek letter sorority and fraternity culture, it was taboo to share your interests publicly. I didn't know any better then, so I said, "Yes!"

"Awesome! You should get to know my sorors," she screeched excitedly.

I assumed by "sorors," she meant the other members of her sorority. She was so nice and sweet about it. I thought, *Oh, wow! This is so cool!* That night, the Cutie Pie Posse and I went to the "study hall." I told them about my experience with my RA earlier, and they thought it was cool, too, as if we had an inside scoop on everything. Little did we know that night would be the last night that we would be known as the Get-Along Gang or the Cutie Pie Posse or be a "crew" any longer. That night, the dynamics of our quartet would change forever.

When we got to the study hall room, I sat near my RA since I "knew" her. A few minutes after study hall started, the crew and I were giggling as we often did when we shared classes. My RA turned and smiled at me and asked me to come sit next to her. She was still smiling, but there was this slightly sinister tone when she said, "Did you do what I told you to do?" I was a little confused. One because of the change in the atmosphere at that moment and two because I honestly had no clue what she was talking about. She turned to one of her "sorors" and said, "Oh, she doesn't remember what I told her." She looked back at me and said, "You need to get every last one of our phone numbers, call us and get to know us." Because I am on the lighter end of the skin tone scale for African American women, I am sure all the color in my face left. However, regardless of my skin tone, I believe the same would have happened at that moment. A sort of fear rose up in me that I wasn't quite familiar with. I had to initiate a conversation with a total stranger AND get their number. With a slight shake in my hand, I tapped the shoulder of the "soror" in front of me. She turned around with that same smile that now felt more like a Chucky doll from the horror classic that came out around that time. I forced out, "Hi, I'm Ereka, and you are?" She said her name. "Would you mind if I got your number and call you sometime?" I felt like I was trying to get a date. "No!" She smiled and turned back around. My heart sank. I wasn't sure what to do with that. I looked at my RA with watering eyes. All she could do was remind me of the assignment. I could still hear the Posse giggling behind me, completely oblivious to what was happening before them. The girl eventually gave me her number after I asked again. I told the crew what happened later that night. I think we all were a little "shook" (slang for shaken), but that night set me on a path of performance, never again to feel that way, the sting of rejection. No, instead of rejection, I was going to prove I was worthy of being chosen.

I could not pledge the sorority that semester because of a lack of money but mostly because of fear. It didn't matter, though, because the cat was out of the bag. *They* knew I was "interested," and for the next couple of years, I would do anything and everything *they* said to prove I was good enough.

Making a Covenant with a Counterfeit

My roommate pledged that semester. The rest of the Posse was happy for her, but deep down, we wish it had been us. The following semester, the Posse started

going our separate ways. The one who was now a sorority member hung out with her sorors. One of the posse
members got a new roommate and had a whole new
crew. The two of us that were left became the best of
friends to this day. We were all we had left.

One day, I got a call from my old roommate, and I
needed to meet at a specific address at a specific time. My
posse BFF got the call, too, and we drove over together. I
was scared out of my mind. I didn't know what to expect.
There were six other girls there when we arrived, along
with my old roommate and all her sorors. We were each
called one by one into the back room while the rest of
the non-sorors looked at each other, recognizing each
other from some of the events we attended but also with
the same look of *what in the heck was about to happen.*
When it was my turn to go in the room, I opened the
door to a dark room with a flashlight pointed in front
of the closet where I was told to stand. For the next few
minutes, I guess you can say I was interviewed. I don't
remember much, except I made the mistake of referring
to the sorority sisters as "sorors," not realizing that was a
reserved word for members only.

I could have thrown up right then. Fortunately, I
made it out alive. It took two years for the sorority to
officially get permission to pledge another line. Still, the
few of us who met that night were already being "initiated" in the interim. They called it being "underground"

because the chapter could be suspended if anyone found out. When they called, I answered, regardless of the time of day. I walked around campus looking over my shoulder like I was running from the mob. I kept telling myself that this was what I needed to do to change my life. I had never tried out for anything in the past because of fear, and this was the closest I had ever gotten to doing something. Being *something*.

The sorority had their "rush," which is the official meeting where you find out what you need to do to pledge the sorority and get an official application package. By this time, I was a pro. I knew all the right things to say and to do. The "underground" line had the inside scoop on everything needed to complete the application. Coming to rush for us was simply a formality. The other girls and I grew close. Who knew shared fear could bond a group of people so well? When it came to the interview process, I had a whole out-of-body experience. I had never done anything like it before. Even when I interviewed for my summer internship with IBM, it was a one-on-one "conversation" with my guidance counselor. I didn't even realize it was an interview until after I was offered the job. I wore my one good suit. A navy-blue skirt and blazer set with gold nautical buttons. I sat at the end of a long table with some of the meanest-looking women staring back at me. There was a mixture of older ladies who I later found out were members of the graduate chapter of the sorority and the four undergraduate members who were left after the two-year "hiatus." They asked me some questions about my volunteer experience. I remember rambling about some Junior Achievement program from junior high, and suddenly, I left, like I left my body. From an aerial view, I was looking at myself and seeing the looks of every person in the room looking back at me. A couple of people smiled to encourage me, but the rest looked like this was the dumbest thing they had heard all day. I am not sure how long the interview lasted, but afterward, I ran to the restroom and bawled. I thought I blew it. I had blown my one chance to become someone else.

I found out later they got a good laugh that day but still selected me for the line. There were 21 of us, including myself and the other two Cutie Pie Posse members. The "formal" process wasn't quite what I expected. I kept telling myself, *This is what is required to wear the letters and stroll at the parties.* On the day of the induction ceremony, we all had on white. I don't remember much about that day because our "big sisters," the current members of the sorority, had us up all night the night before. It's called "hell" night in Greek culture and is supposed to be the longest and hardest night of the entire process. Oddly enough, I had a ball. I was teaching my line sisters steps that I learned volunteering at this community center, and we were practicing for our "coming out" show, which is when you get to publicly announce to the world that you are now a member of the sorority by putting on a mini step show. What I do remember about that day is kneeling on a pillow by candlelight, signing my name on a piece of paper containing the words "lifetime commitment," and reciting an oath to pledge my life to the sorority. I thought it was the strangest thing and almost spooky. I kept thinking, "Did 'they' go through this?" Thinking about my ex-roommate and her line sisters when they pledged two years prior. This wasn't strolling at parties and having everyone look at you with respect and awe. This was something different. Nonetheless, I did it. I signed. I committed. I came into agreement. I made the exchange.

CHAPTER 3

THE TRUTH

After the ceremony, we had a big ole party at Ryan's Steakhouse. There was a whole table dedicated to each of us, full of Greek paraphernalia with our line numbers and line names on them. I felt like I was finally accepted. I have my "sisters" who are going to have my back. I am somebody now. That feeling was short-lived. A few weeks after becoming a member, we had our first "lemon squeeze." We were told this was where you come to air your dirty laundry and settle your grievances with another sister because you never want to expose all of that in public. In public, regardless, you present a united front. I thought, okay, makes sense. The big sisters went around the room and shared their grievances with each one of my line sisters.

When they got to me, one said, "You just need to lose weight." I was a little confused because I thought I was "accepted." They chose me when I was this size, so why was she saying something was wrong with it? What was even more messed up was when they got to one of my line sisters, who was probably the same size as me, they told her she was perfect just as she was. I couldn't understand it. What made me so much different from her? There I was, thinking that I had finally been accepted for exactly who I was, but only to find out it was all a lie. They began to tell me how I needed to dress, how I needed to act, and even how I needed to talk. As a member of the sorority, there were things that you could do, and there were definitely things that you were forbidden to do. There were so many restrictions and conforming things; to be independent was to be rebellious, and you would be ostracized. Everything was happening so fast that one minute, I was overjoyed that I had this opportunity to be a part of this group that I thought would always support me and have my back, only to find out in the next minute that what I envisioned was not it at all.

A Counterfeit Identity

I was a quick study, though. I learned how to dress, how to act, and even how to feel. I still felt insecure on the inside, but the way people responded to me on the outside made up for it. The approving looks I got when I was on campus it was like wearing those Greek letters across my chest camouflaged my "fatness." My line sisters and I ordered these bright yellow matching jackets with our line names and numbers on them. We all wore them to school on the same day, and we were the talk of the school. It was like we had this superpower. Every girl wanted to be us, and every guy wanted to be with us. Even me. I had my first boyfriend. He wasn't a student. He worked at the school, but it didn't matter. For the first time, I was an "it" girl. I was part of the "cool" crowd. When I went to parties, I danced amongst my sisters, and when we strolled, I felt alive and free. I was finally "somebody."

It was a different story when it came to being around the big sisters, including the ones who pledged our chapter before us or members from other chapters. They already had the "superpower," so we were on the same playing field. I always felt like I had to prove something to be accepted by them. Even though I was a member, I still felt like I was pledging when it came to them. It was the same way when it came to the brother fraternity. There was one of two ways that they would "accept" you. You got in good with them with your femininity/sex appeal or toughness. Naturally, I was neither. So, to keep from being considered "cat" or not cool, I chose to act tough. I literally wrestled dudes twice my size. I loathed going to events where I was going to encounter them. I was always on alert to respond with words or actions to defend myself. Proving that I was not "cat." It was literally and figuratively exhausting. I always felt like it was harder being a member of the sorority than the process of becoming one.

After about two years, several of my line sisters had graduated college and moved on with their lives, so only a handful of us were left in the undergraduate chapter. We knew it was time to pledge a new line, and we did what we were taught. We identified some girls who were always attending our events and got them together one night. The problem was, even though my line sisters and I put up a united front in public, we were severely divided behind closed doors. We eventually cliqued up (separated into two dominant groups). I will refer to them as Team A and Team B to eliminate confusion. I was on Team A, which consisted of current students. Team B included one student, and the rest were alumni. Team A met with the "interested" girls one night without inviting or informing Team B. Team B found out and decided to have their own "meeting" with the girls. Team A found out what Team B had done, and let's just say all hell broke loose. Once the smoke cleared, the chapter and several members of Team B were suspended, and it would be two more years before a new group of girls could be initiated. Not only were relationships ruined, but lives were ruined. Even though I have restored some of those relationships, it still pains me to this day to know the role I played in causing so much pain.

Because there was no "fresh meat" in the sorority at our school, the ones who were left had to "represent" at every event, every meeting, everything. Not to mention the out-of-town events, like other school homecomings, and we can't forget the step shows. Stepping became one of my favorite things. I remember the first step show I competed in. We practiced well into the wee hours of the morning, but I didn't mind. Stepping was like dancing to me. It was choreographed moves with some parts set to music. I loved it. Since only a few of us were left on campus, no one thought we could pull it off. The day of the show, I was so nervous. I felt like all eyes would be on me because I was the "big girl." Once the beat dropped to '90s rapper Mystikal's "Here I Go," the nerves were gone. I decided at that moment that if all eyes were going to be on me, I would give them something to look at. We came in second place that night, but my confidence level was on a thousand. People approached me all night, saying they had no clue I could step. It was like this was the moment I had been waiting for. The moment when I got to show the world what I could do.

Even though most of us had graduated, we were considered the last remaining members on the campus and treated like royalty. We were known on our college campus and throughout the southeast region. There was nowhere that we wouldn't go. No campus that we wouldn't boldly step on. I remember one of my other line sisters saw me and said every guy she met from the brother fraternity knew me no matter where she went. I wasn't referred to as the "fat girl" anymore. I was just "that girl."

One day, we went out to eat after a party. It was the fast-food hangout that everyone went to after every event because they were open 24 hours. This guy approached my line sister, and she was not interested. He became verbally aggressive. I stepped in to defend her, and he started calling me names. "Fat this… fat that." I looked around for "backup," but no one came. Fear crept in. He didn't care that I was in the sorority. He wasn't from our school. He didn't know me as "that girl." He eventually left us alone, but for that brief moment, I was taken back to before. The same insecure, shy, fearful, fat girl. The thing about confidence is that if it is not born from the inside, it can easily be shaken.

After four years and with only one member left in the undergraduate chapter, we finally got permission to pledge a line. A lot of things had changed in my personal life. I went through my first break-up and experienced heartbreak for the first time. I had also given my life to the Lord and joined a local church. Even though I had become a "Christian," I was still a sorority girl, and since the sorority was founded on "Christian" principles, I didn't see an issue. Because I had already graduated college, I joined the graduate chapter of the sorority so I could participate in the pledge process. I was working a full-time job, but I wanted to do my part in helping pledge this new line. I talked to members from different chapters to ask about their pledge process and totally reformed our process. I learned along the way that the pledging process was to strip a person down from who they thought they were and build them into a member of the sorority. That was your new identity, and that was who you would be. In the short amount of time that we spent with them, the goal was to create a bond of sisterhood between the girls by creating these shared experiences.

I treated those girls like they were my own children. I didn't want them to feel like I did after pledging. I wanted them to feel empowered. It worked, too. You couldn't tell those girls anything after they "crossed" over into membership in the sorority. Even the ones who were the least likely candidates had attitude. LOL. I was very protective of them, too. If I felt like one of the brother fraternity members was challenging them to see if they were "cat," I was quick to defend them. I felt like they were a reflection of me and calling them "cat" was like calling me "cat," and I couldn't have that. Instead of being the one who had to prove myself, I had to make sure these new girls lived up to the image. There was one incident where I and a few of my line sisters got dressed for a party without seeing each other beforehand. We all showed up wearing similar colors and similar styles and looking similar. One of the new initiates came to the party wearing a floral dress. I asked her what she was wearing.

"A dress with flowers. I love flowers," she uttered.

I scolded her, "Do you see us in flowers?"

"No," her voice shook.

"That's because we don't wear flowers. Now go home and take it off."

Acting like that didn't make me feel good. Something felt off about it, but I was perpetuating a lie. I had done it for so long and gone so far that I pushed it to the back of my mind and kept it moving. This was *just the way*, I thought.

Eventually, the new girls came into their own. They didn't need us to show them the way anymore. My line sisters and I had become old news. Our phones were not ringing to attend the latest events. Things got quiet.

The Unveiling

I didn't realize then, but God was intentionally putting space between me and the sorority. He was putting space between me and a lot of things. I decided to get more involved with the graduate chapter so I could still do things with the sorority. At the same time, I got more involved with my church. I didn't grow up in church, so I felt I had to play catch up. I was a part of everything at church: the choir, the teen ministry, and the young adult ministry. My commitment to the church and God was everything to me. One day, the church was having an event that happened to be on the same day as a sorority event. Since I couldn't do both and I couldn't let down the church or God, I told the sorority that I wouldn't be able to make their event. Well, I ended up getting a call from the graduate chapter president. She told me, "I know you got church, and that's all good, but you know, this sorority, this is a lifetime commitment." I stared at the phone, not believing what I was hearing. Because what I thought I heard was this lady asking me to choose the sorority over God. I was new in my faith, but something didn't sit well with me regarding her comment. After that, I stopped my involvement with the graduate chapter altogether.

With the sorority life more on the back burner, I focused on my faith. I learned that God created me for a purpose, and I believed a part of that purpose had to do with what I did for a living. I'd graduated with an electrical engineering degree and started working at IBM shortly after graduation. There was always this creative part of me that I explored as a hobby. I designed flyers for the sorority events. While working at IBM, I learned the basics of web design. I started playing around with different programs and combining what I was learning in graphic design and web design, and I loved it. I felt like God was with me when I was designing. These ideas would just come to me as I sat in front of a blank canvas. I felt web design was the perfect marriage between my creative and technical sides. We were asked what our spiritual gifts were during a meeting for our young adult ministry at my church. I heard the words teacher, preacher, evangelist, etc. When I was asked about it, I said it was web design. There was a chuckle in the room, and I was told it had to be one of the five-fold ministries (teacher, pastor, evangelist, prophet, apostle). Since I was "new" to all this, I just filed it in the back of my mind, but I couldn't shake the feeling of being called to do more than what I was doing at my job. So, I ended up resigning my job. I believed I had to take a chance on what I believed God was showing me. I later discovered that few people were "stepping out on faith" like that. Even my pastor at the time said God would never tell someone to leave their job without having another lined up. I stayed at my job for another month before I actually left. A couple of weeks before my last day, I started to get cold feet, but my boss said they had hired someone else for the position. I had no choice at that point. I was going to have to make the leap. Funny enough, I found out later that no one ever replaced me at my job. I subsequently ended up moving back to West Palm Beach with my family.

Now that I was physically separated from sorority life, it slowly became a thing of "out of sight, out of mind." It was only when my line sister bestie called me about the current line that was being initiated at the undergraduate chapter that I realized how detached I was. She was upset because she felt the current undergraduate members were keeping secrets about what was happening with the new pledges and not letting her be involved. I shrugged my shoulders and sighed on the phone. Not that I was not sympathetic to how she felt, but I really couldn't have cared less about what was going on with them and had no desire to be involved. I told her she might also want to detach because I felt nothing. Nothing at all. Whereas a year prior, I would have been right there with her.

Because I was emotionally detached, I started to see little things. I remember going to church after I moved back home, and one of the older church members found out I was also a sorority member. She grabbed me and "challenged me" with the secret handshake to prove that I was a member right in the middle of a meet-and-greet during the Sunday church service. I thought, *how strange that she would even care about that stuff, being a Christian and a grown woman at that.*

I was in this discovery phase of knowing who I was and doing the work that I felt I needed to do to "become." I tried losing weight and working out, but I wasn't consistent. One day, a lady at church who lost a lot of weight became a coach and held an interest meeting. At first, I wasn't going to go; for me, it was shame. It was like if I ignored the problem, I didn't have to feel shame. I also felt that God was giving me an opportunity, and I didn't want it to pass me by. I signed up and ended up losing 60 pounds. Even though I could wear smaller clothes and shop in different stores, I still saw myself the same.

I was in West Palm for about six years before the Lord spoke to my heart about moving to Atlanta. I didn't jump at the chance to leave, but I knew God was trying to reveal something to me, and my current environment did not foster that. I was reminded when God told Abraham to leave his family and go to a place that He would show him, and in doing so, He was able to show Abraham His vision for him. I was at this place where I wanted to know my purpose in life, and if Atlanta had the answers, I was open to going.

Before I decided to move, I visited Atlanta to "scout the land," so to speak. Once I got there, I had lunch with a few of my line sisters who were living there at the time. I wasn't sure of their religious beliefs, so I kept the conversation light around my potential move. One of my line sisters started sharing what God was doing in her life and how she didn't have a job because God had told her to leave the practice of law. She didn't really understand, but she wanted to be obedient. I was all ears at that point because someone else was speaking my language. I didn't think God was telling others to do "crazy" things like I felt He was telling me. That day, I heard something different in my line sister that would connect us for the rest of our lives.

It took me about a year later to be obedient and make the move. Because of what my pastor said, I proposed to my then-employer that I work remotely once I moved. I ended up getting fired instead. At the time of this writing, working remotely is a common way of life. Back then, it was not. They couldn't even give me a reason as to why they were letting me go. I had no other excuses preventing me from packing up and moving to Atlanta. A few months later, I headed to Atlanta in my neatly packed car, without knowing what was in store for me.

DELIVERANCE

I ended up moving in with my line sister, who left the practice of law and whom I will refer to as my spirit sister. Neither of us had a job at that point, and we were trying to figure out what God was trying to say to us. I had no clue about the adventure we were about to embark on but looking back, I would have to describe it as magical. It was a season of eye-opening, jaw-dropping revelation and a test of our faith. One day, we were conversing about confidence, and I said when I was with my sorority line sisters, I felt confident and bold. I knew they had my back, and that's how I showed up. I showed up with this kind of boldness. And my spirit sister said to me, "Ereka, the Lord wants that for you. He wants to be that for you. He wants you to experience that not because of somebody else but because of Him." That kind of sat with me for a little while, and I guess it stayed in the back of my mind. I never leaned more into what that really meant or what that could feel like. In all honesty, at that time, there had been such a separation between me and some of my line sisters because of the incident that happened in college that there was no communication with them. Because I was in this space of seeking the Lord and finding out His will for my life, He started speaking to me about forgiveness. And He had me reach out to each of my line sisters, those I wasn't close to, and ask them for their forgiveness. Not seek forgiveness from them but ask them for their forgiveness and apologize for my role in our separation. And once that happened, we started talking again. It wasn't to the level it had been in the past, but it was a start.

The Awakening

My spirit sister invited me to enroll in a spiritual warfare class that her church was offering. Now, growing up, I was always considered "scary." Have you ever heard the saying, "You are so scary that you jump at your own shadow?" Yeah, that was me. So, the thought of talking about demons or anything like that wasn't a conversation I wanted to have. I was even afraid to read about demons in the Bible. Like, I literally was afraid to read the Bible, people!

Nonetheless, I decided to take the class. I was blown away by what I learned. I got clarity about what spiritual warfare was and was not. You see, the enemy of God is Satan, which makes him our enemy. According to John 10:10, the enemy's plan is to "steal, kill, and destroy." We can knowingly or unknowingly come into agreement with the enemy's plan against us when we make vows, pledges, and covenants with darkness.

One day, my spirit sister came to me after rereading our sorority "rituals." These were the books we were given after we were initiated into the sorority. The books contained all of the ceremonies and meeting rituals that every member of the organization performed. She read the contract we signed all those years ago when we were kneeling on that pillow in the dark next to that burning candle. We signed our name to a pledge that committed us for a lifetime to an organization. On the surface, it wasn't so bad, but when God showed us that we pledged our lives to an idol, that's when we freaked out.

We were like, "Oh my God!" We pledged our lives and devotion to something we knew nothing about. Spiritually, it was an exchange. It was like we were at an altar exchanging our lives. We made an oath to an idol. The Bible says, "Thou shall have no other gods before

Me." Exodus 20:3 KJV. We knew we had to renounce that oath. We had to break that agreement. I know some of you may be reading this and rolling your eyes, thinking *please, it is not that deep. They are just words.* You may think that, and that's fine. I believe God gives us revelation about things when we're ready for them, and at that time, I was ready. God started revealing to me how I did make an exchange because I wasn't confident in who He created me to be. Even though I hadn't been associated with the sorority in years, it was really hard to let go of the idea of being a "member." I felt like my membership made me somebody. My spirit sister was the first to renounce, but it was still a struggle for me. I had built so much of my identity around the sorority. I mean, I was known. People knew who I was without me knowing them. It was like I was giving up things I loved, like stepping. Oh my gosh, I know I've said it several times, but I loved to step. I wrestled with it for a while until the Lord started showing me the truth, that I wasn't losing anything but gaining so much more. "You're gaining authentic confidence. You're gaining who you really are. The opportunity to be introduced to the 'real' you," He whispered in my spirit. This required me to shed those false ideas about myself, those counterfeits I had come into agreement with that I thought made me somebody. I had to break the covenant I made with a counterfeit identity and begin the journey to discover who God created me to be.

Breaking the Covenant

I made the decision to break the covenant. My spirit sister walked me through the process that God showed her. She said that when we come into agreement with the enemy, we give him a legal right and access to our lives. Repentance renders that agreement null and void. It strips the enemy of that right. We then have the authority to break that agreement. I did just that. I repented, broke the agreement, and committed my life to the Lord. My spirit sister had written an email to all of our line sisters letting them know that she had renounced the sorority, and a few weeks after, I followed suit. I am not sure how I expected any of them to respond. I guess it wasn't much of a shock since my spirit sister had sent her email prior. I got a call from one of my line sisters, who was close to me and also a believer in Christ. She said she was calling on behalf of the others, but they were concerned as to why I felt God would tell me to do something like that and hadn't spoken to any of them. I responded, "I don't know why. I just know that I can't ignore it."

I isolated myself after that. There was this fear of having to justify the choice to renounce the sorority. I never publicly shared it with anyone outside my sisters. This part of me still questioned whether I made the right decision. I felt what I believed others thought: was it really *that deep*? I avoided events where I knew people who knew me from college would be. I felt the best way to avoid any confrontation was to go off the grid. I would still have dreams about stepping at parties. Because my love for dance was limited to stepping or strolling at parties and other events that associated me with the sorority, I stopped dancing as well. I took 2 Corinthians 5:17 literally. Since I was this new creature in Christ, I had to let go of everything about my old life.

That was a very difficult season to navigate. I was in a place where I didn't know who I was anymore and was trying to figure it out. I found myself reverting back to what was familiar. I became quiet and reserved. I stayed in the background to avoid hurt. My identity was again in question.

REFLECTION

Being in that place of not knowing who I was, opened me up to all types of counterfeits. Some counterfeits are not as obvious as others. A counterfeit can show up to fill a void, like counterfeit relationships, counterfeit religion, or counterfeit love. It's not that it's bad in and of itself; it's just not God's best.

In reading my story and the path that led me to recognize that I'd made a covenant with a counterfeit, I hope that you have been able to identify some areas in your own life that need to be explored. The beauty of this journey is that you don't take it alone. God wants to take the journey with you. It is His heart for you to be free to BE, and it is through relationship with Him that you have the access to do that.

It's time to pause and reflect so that you can sit with God (Father, Jesus, and Holy Spirit) to identify the counterfeits in your life. Ask Him the questions below. Remember the first-word principle and write down the first words you hear in response. I recommend writing in a journal in addition to the space provided.

*Have I believed something about myself
that You did not say about me?*

_____

_____

_____

_____

_____

What is the lie?

_____

_____

_____

_____

_____

_____

_____

_____

_____

_____

_____

When did I first believe this lie?

_____

_____

_____

_____

What is the truth that You want me to know?

_____

_____

_____

_____

_____

_____

_____

_____

_____

_____

_____

CHAPTER 5

THE AUTHENTICITY ADVANTAGE

I was in Atlanta for seven years before I moved back home to West Palm Beach. I would have to define that season in Atlanta as "enough is enough." Because I didn't have a job, I took that time to work on my business and try my hand at entrepreneurship full-time. I learned some hard life lessons in business that were catalysts to some of the most defining moments in my life. What I learned in that season about myself was I was looking externally for validation from relationships, church, positions, clients, etc., trying to find which one clicked. I felt like a chameleon. I learned to blend in with the environment. I stayed in the background to play it safe and became a shadow of what was happening around me. What I received in return was heartbreak, burnout, church hurt, and shame.

I was approaching my 40th birthday, and there was this moment, like a light bulb went off in my head, when I came to the conclusion that I didn't want to live life based on what other people thought of me. I did not want to spend the next 40 years as I did the first. Things didn't start to shift immediately, but I was more intentional about it.

Once I moved back to West Palm, little things started to change, like wearing sleeveless shirts. *What does "sleeveless shirts" have to do with anything you ask?* I used to be ashamed of the stretch marks on my arms, so I covered them up. I moved back to West Palm Beach in August of 2014, and I honestly couldn't remember it being that hot. I went out and bought a bunch of sleeveless shirts and refused to die of heat stroke because of fear of being teased.

In January 2020, I prayed about the new year and what to expect. What I felt in my spirit was the Lord saying that by the end of the year, I wouldn't be able to recognize myself. That He wanted my outside to reflect my inside. I had no clue that in just a couple of months, God would push a reset button on the world, and our entire way of life would shift drastically. The coronavirus pandemic caused a global shutdown, and I went through a personal shutdown and restart. I started working with an image consultant because I knew I would need help if my outside was going to change. What I thought was going to be a wardrobe transformation turned out to be a process of inner healing and discovery. I also knew I would leave my job and start the business thing again that year. I didn't want to repeat my past mistakes with business. I was introduced to Kingdom Driven Entrepreneurs (KDE), which is a community of believers that partner with God to align with His heart in their business and understand their kingdom identity and assignment. I signed up for their mentoring program because I knew I needed help understanding how to do business and wanted to know how to do it God's way. I was partnered with a mentor who was also in the branding space. I thought I was just there to learn how to do business God's way, but every session led me back to God and having conversations about my relationship with Him. I was getting a little frustrated because I was there to learn about business. What I came to understand is that partnering with God in business is developed by a relationship with God. I thought my relationship was fine, but with God, there is always more. The result was I started to grow in my relationship with God and understand His heart for me. Who He created me to be. How He wired me. I started to dispel lies that I believed about myself. It's not that I hadn't experienced deliverance and inner healing before, but what I realized is that I spent a lot of time trying to modify my behavior. But that season showed me how to address the issue at the root. To ask God where these beliefs about myself stemmed from. God was uprooting a faulty foundation in my beliefs about Him, myself, and what He had called me to do and to align with His truth.

My KDE mentor was set to speak at a virtual summit hosted by Dr. Eboni L. Truss in the spring of 2020. Since everything went virtual during this time and I was working my full-time job from home, as was everyone else in the world, I was able to attend the summit. I signed up for the bonus to catch the replays because I knew I couldn't engage fully and work. There were a host of other speakers, including quite a few from the KDE community. I was blown away by what I heard that day. The ideas seemed radical from what I heard in the church, but they aligned with my spirit. Understanding that my business is not just what I do but a means of expression of who God created me to be, I started following the speakers on social media and signing up for programs they were offering. One of which was "Brand with Grace," which my KDE mentor was offering.

While in this program, some of my life's breadcrumbs started to piece together. During the first session, who popped up on the virtual screen but none other than Dr. Eboni. Something in my spirit said to pay attention to her. That there was a reason why we were in this class together. During the class, we would get homework assignments with questions to sit with God about. During one of the sessions, Dr. Eboni got the revelation of Un-Becoming. She said God showed her that we spend our lives trying to *become* someone when God created us to *be* from the foundation of the world. She talked about how, in business, we copy the blueprint of the gurus when God has a blueprint from heaven specifically designed for us. Something in what she said struck me. Not because I was prone to copying the blueprint of business gurus but because she had the language to explain what I had been feeling all my life. I was on Dr. Eboni's mailing list because I had signed up for the virtual summit she hosted. So, a few weeks after she shared her revelation in class, I got an email about her holding an information session. I signed up to attend, and during the session, she shared about an offering she was going to have the next year. I prayed about whether I was supposed to join the 6-month program, and God said to sign up for the next cohort. I told Dr. Eboni what I believed God said, and she was blown away because she didn't even know if she would have a second cohort. What was included in the registration was a 90-minute Prophetic

Business Intensive (PBI) where Dr. Eboni would walk you through hearing from God about your business. I scheduled my appointment. About a week or so before the session, a friend told me about the movie *Harriet* and how I needed to watch it. I was hesitant at first because I don't like movies about slavery because I get angry about the way African Americans were treated. She said I really needed to watch it, and so I did. The first scene caught my attention right away because Harriet was having visions. I soon learned that she was hearing from God, and He would show her visions of things that would happen in the future. When she escaped from slavery and made her way to freedom, she gave the credit to God. In the movie, she said God led her, but it was her feet that did the walking. A year after she was living as a free woman, God was giving her visions about going back and helping others, even in the face of risking her own safety. There was a scene where she was leading a group of people to freedom, and they came to a river. Everybody with her thought she was crazy and wanted to turn and go another way, but God showed her there was danger in the other direction, and this was the only way. She stepped into the river and paused halfway through with the water up to her chin, not knowing if she would go under. She said, "Rivers of living water flow through me. God help me to cross." She stepped forward and started to go up again. I heard in my spirit so clearly *that's what you will do.* I wailed. One because I knew God was speaking to me and two because of fear. The thought of leading people scared me. I felt like Gideon in the book of Judges when God called him a mighty man of valor, and Gideon basically said," What you talking bout, Willis? I shared what God said during my PBI with Dr. Eboni. I shared briefly all the moments of my life that had gotten me to this point and wanted clarity about what God had called me to do. To say our time together was intense would be an understatement. She basically confirmed what God said about me being a Harriet. She said I had a "Harriet anointing" on my life. The same one that Jesus had to set the captives free. Whether that was helping someone figure out what was wrong with their website or their marriage. She helped uncover fears that stemmed from childhood that centered around rejection and perfectionism. The level of healing that took place in that one encounter was transformational. Holy Spirit brought back so many memories during that session that confirmed who I'd been my entire life. I realized I spent so much time trying to figure out what God had called me to do that I overlooked who He created me to Be.

The Creator knows His creation inside and out. It's on us to take the time to ask. What would stop me from asking, you say? Believing a lie about God and myself. What God showed me is that my life as I had known it was built on a faulty foundation…a counterfeit, and He wanted to restore, renew, and realign me to His heart for me.

Pillar One: God Loves Me

When it comes to understanding your identity and who God created you to be, it starts with knowing God and, more importantly, knowing God loves you. *God loves me* seems so elementary when it comes to our faith, but knowing this truth in the fullness of the revelation is vital to living a life in alignment and fulfillment with God. When you truly believe this, the decisions you make and the actions you take reflect it. Because I'd grown up under a lot of criticism, I also looked at God that way. I remember saying that I wished He would just give me a playbook so I could run the plays exactly as He wished. I wanted to know things beforehand so I could control the outcome. You can't get it wrong if you can plan ahead. I was a stickler for getting it right the first time. I viewed correction as punishment and wanted to prevent correction as much as possible. I came to realize that was impossible. I soon learned that perfection was also impossible.

I attributed God's love for me based on how well I could perform. If I did things right, God would love me and, therefore, would bless me. When things were not going well, I believed I had done something wrong and needed to fix it. The way I viewed God affected how I viewed myself. I was always trying to figure out how to get it right. My relationship with God was similar to that of a lot of other believers, transactional. If I do this, then God will do this. That couldn't be further from the truth. The truth is God created us for love. For His good pleasure. Before the foundation of the world, He made me His beloved. He is a good Father, and His love is unconditional regardless of what I do or don't do. Whether I'm right or wrong, I am still loved.

There was a big fear that God was going to disappoint me. He reminded me of an incident as a child that left me heartbroken. It was my first heartbreak when someone I loved disappointed me. That was an unconscious fear I had of God. That He was like that. So, every time I experienced disappointment, I blamed God. Not myself, or the choices of others, but God. I had the opportunity to experience the truth of God's love over a series of encounters. There was one time when God had me go back to the incident when my heart was first broken because of disappointment, and I asked where He was. I saw Jesus sitting beside me at that moment, rubbing my back and comforting me. He showed me all the things that were in play at that moment and things I didn't realize were going on as a child. It changed my whole perspective of the incident. It no longer made me sad. I was able to have compassion towards those who caused the wound and was able to forgive and truly let it go. That was such a pivotal moment in my relationship with God. Now, I ask Him to show me things from His perspective. When we see God, ourselves, and others from a fractured lens, it affects our lives in so many ways.

REFLECTION

Here are some prompts to ask God. Remember the first word principle.

God, how would You describe my relationship with You?

_____

_____

_____

_____

_____

What have I believed about You that is not true?

_____

_____

_____

_____

_____

_____

_____

_____

What is the truth You want me to know?

Pillar Two: I Am Who He Says I Am

My relationship with God began to flourish. I started to receive God's love in ways I had not allowed Him to pour into me before. My beliefs about God shifted. I realized that there was no earthly comparison to God's love. Yes, He can love us through others, and His love even exceeds that. Any good relationship requires cultivation. It's not a one-and-done experience. My relationship with the Lord went from experience to experience to moment by moment. I started to trust God truly; because I trusted Him, I could believe who He said I was created to be.

My style coach scheduled a photo shoot for me in Atlanta to culminate my year of transformation. She picked out clothes for me. Set me up with a hair and make-up artist and arranged a session with a photographer. I believe God was preparing me for this time of coming out from behind the shadows, which aligns with what He said earlier about my outside reflecting my inside. I was so nervous that weekend in December when I got to Atlanta. I was afraid the clothes that she picked wouldn't fit. The hairstyle wouldn't look right. So many things were going on in my head, but I found a place of rest. I surrendered it all to God. My first stop was to my stylist to try on the clothes she got. I was not feeling some of the stuff, so she promised to bring more stuff later that night. She stopped by, and I tried on a few other things. They just didn't fit "me." I didn't want to be someone else in those pictures. I had spent most of my life fantasizing that I was someone else. One thing I told the Lord was that if He was going to put me out in the front, I had to be okay with being me.

The day of the shoot, I got up early and headed to the hair stylist who was also going to do my makeup. We decided to lighten my hair and go with a tapered cut to my natural hair. I left that salon in shock. I kept looking at myself like, WHAT! It was me, but my makeup was flawless; it wasn't too much, either. I was so ME just on 1000.

When I got to the shoot, my stylist couldn't believe her eyes. I felt like Cinderella showing up to the ball. When she pulled out the clothes, there was one shirt that she said Holy Spirit told her to pick up that morning. I almost cried when I saw it. It was rainbow-colored with sequins. It went perfectly with the teal, yellow, and fuchsia Converse® I bought. This outfit was my personality manifested in clothes.

I had a "confidence" coach on set who helped pose me. I still felt awkward taking the pictures because I never liked wearing heels, and one of the outfits was paired with some really high ones. I was also in my head, not wanting my back rolls or the stretch marks on my legs to show. It was a whole thing until a moment that changed everything. My confidence coach was posing me in a red and black pantsuit. She could sense that I felt awkward. She stopped the shoot and asked the photographer to show me one of the pictures. When I looked at the camera, I was like, *who is that?* That picture was fire! They all shouted, "That's you!" The next photo I took became my signature photo. They were saying I started to feel it. I started to believe. I saw how God orchestrated every moment up until that point, and then we were there, capturing it on film. When I looked into the camera, I was no longer thinking about how I looked. I was focused on what He promised at the beginning of the year. I decided at that moment to own all of me.

REFLECTION

Who has God said He created you to be? Let's ask the questions:

God, who have You created me to be?

_____

_____

_____

_____

_____

_____

_____

What have You said about me that I didn't believe?

_____

_____

_____

_____

_____

_____

What, if anything, is hindering me from believing all of who You say that I am?

CHAPTER 6

REDEMPTION

On New Year's Day 2021, I posted the pictures I took during the shoot on Facebook with the following caption:

> *"So I am not a resolution type person but I do ask the Lord what He has to say about what the new year is supposed to look like for me. Last year He said, "Daughter, by the end of the year, you won't recognize yourself." Then He said, "I want your outside to reflect what you look like on the inside." I had no clue what that meant or what that was going to look like but last year for me was a complete "Unbecoming" as one of my mentors would say. The world was quarantined and God went to work on and in me. My entire life up until this point had been*

playing it safe in the background for fear of what other people would think. What I discovered was the Lord wanted me to be everything He said I was but He wanted me to partner with Him to do it. So I spent most of 2020 discovering my authentic self with the help of coaches, mentors, friends and anyone else that the Lord told me to connect with...

This year the Lord said His word for me is "accelerated elevation". I am not qualified. I have no clue what I am doing. I am still learning who I am daily but the Lord said its [sic] not because of who I am but because of who He is in me. He also said that I would help others walk in freedom just by witnessing my journey. So 2021 is my year to let my (His) light shine. I don't know what its [sic] going to look like when its [sic] all said and done but I am excited to partner with Him on this journey."

I had no clue how prophetic those words would be. Accelerated elevation was an understatement.

The Unveiling - Part II

A couple of weeks after our divine encounter at the diner, Dr. Eboni contacted me about attending a women's retreat that she was hosting. Based on my experiences from other religious-type encounters where we had women's conferences and retreats, I was definitely not interested in going. But after our meeting, she messaged me saying, "I think you're supposed to be there, but pray about it." And so, I kind of had this attitude. I was like, *okay, I'm gonna pray about it.* At the same time, I was telling God, *you know I don't like these kinds of things.* I felt like I was getting a yes to go. I was feeling a little anxious about it because of being in a season of isolation, and there I was going into this environment where there were people I didn't know, and "peopling" was not my jam. Yet, still, I agreed to go. Everything fell into place for me to attend, even though it was last minute. The night before I was supposed to leave, Dr. Eboni called and said, "I think you are supposed to share your testimony at this retreat." I could have thrown up right then and there. I was like, why would I do that? Like, who is coming to this retreat that would need to hear my story? I didn't say anything to her at the time.

I got to the retreat, and I was a nervous wreck. Like I said before, I usually share my testimony one-on-one and only when I am led to share it. By that point, I wasn't much of a public speaker. The thought of talking to people I didn't know literally made me want to hurl. There were 15 ladies at this retreat and only a couple I recognized from meeting them virtually a couple of weeks prior. One was a lady who coined me as her cousin after saying how much I looked like her aunt.

I saw a bag on the bed when I walked into one of the bedrooms. The bag had sorority letters on it. I thought *oh great, now I have to share my story in front of someone who is a member of a sorority.* After spending the day getting to know the ladies, I relaxed and stopped thinking about when I was going to share my story. Everyone was so nice and genuine. I started feeling comfortable and enjoying myself. During one of the first sessions, we had to ask God what He wanted for us at this retreat. Up to that point, I still struggled with whether I was hearing from God. I had learned the first-word principle: to go with the first word you hear as God. What I heard was that God wanted to take the lampshade off me, and I would no longer be hidden. That experience was life-changing for me. That word held true on the second day of the retreat. I went to the restroom, and as I was coming out, I heard Dr. Eboni calling my name, so I eased back in the bathroom because clearly, she could not have been calling me. There were a few of the other ladies sitting in the connecting bedroom. Unbeknownst to me, she called them in while I was using the restroom. Dr. Eboni came in and shut the door. I still didn't understand why I was in the room. Most of the ladies in the room had been facilitators during the retreat. In the early session, we were split up into groups. Dr. Eboni assigned each lady a group and asked us to speak God's heart for the group. I just told you I was struggling with whether I was hearing from God. She turned to me and said she wanted me to speak a word to all the groups. I thought *this lady couldn't possibly know the Lord because why would she ask me of all people? God, if we are going to do this, then You gotta do it. I don't want to be afraid. I just want to be me.* We exited the room, and I shared what came to mind, thinking *this is the dumbest stuff I have ever heard.* To my surprise, they all agreed when the groups were asked if what I said registered. The rest of the weekend was like that. People would stop talking to hear what I had to say. It was the craziest thing ever. That weekend, my life shifted. The lampshade was off, and people could see me. I had the opportunity to come out of my comfort zone and experience what life feels like in the "courage zone," as one of my dear sister-friends coined it.

Something shifted for me right then. It was like this newfound confidence came to me. I was in a safe space, and it was okay to be me. I didn't even consider what Dr. Eboni said about sharing my testimony. Something else happened for me during that retreat. I felt something I hadn't felt before amongst these ladies who embraced me just as I was. That Saturday morning, while looking in the mirror in the bathroom, I realized that those ladies felt like my sisters, and we had only just met. I heard in my spirit "real sisterhood." Authentic sisterhood. I immediately went to look for Dr. Eboni to share the revelation I had gotten, and she said, "Then you should share your testimony tonight at our dinner." My eyes got big because I thought maybe I could slide past that. I still hadn't determined which one of my newfound sisters was a part of a sorority, so I wasn't sure if my testimony would offend them. Nonetheless, I was going to do what I had to do. Even if it scared the mess out of me. There was no way I was going backward.

My "cousin" said I could ride with her and a couple of the other ladies to the restaurant. We pulled up to the restaurant and started walking towards the door. I don't know why, but I glanced back at my cousin's vehicle, and on the front were sorority symbols. My stomach dropped. I didn't want my testimony to make anyone uncomfortable. Especially my newfound cousin. I barely ate my dinner. I didn't even sit next to her. I was dreading the moment that I was going to make things uncomfortable. As we wrapped up dinner, the time came for me to share. I was shaking like a leaf. It was cold in the restaurant, but this was the shiver of fear. As I shared, I glanced over at my cousin to see if she was giving me a mean look, but I got nothing. After I finished sharing, what happened next surprised me. One of the ladies said God spoke to her while I was sharing, and it served as confirmation for her to separate from a business she was a part of.

I was thinking, *Really, you got that out of what I said?* Wow. That opened the floor to different questions that people had about religious organizations they or family members belonged to and wanted to know if those were covenants that they needed to break. Everyone was talking, but I wasn't getting much from my cousin, and she was the one that I cared most about how she felt. Once we got in the car, I got a text from her. "We need to talk." I thought, *Man, I'm about to lose this relationship with my newfound cousin.*

Later that night, we went into one of the rooms. She spoke, "Cousin… I need you to walk me through renouncing the sorority." I was shocked. For some reason, I thought she was going to be mad with me, but here she was, asking me to walk her through the process. She said God told her to break it, and I was grateful for the opportunity to help her.

I was blown away at how these strangers came together and experienced God together. We experienced His love together and individually. I got to encounter God in a whole new way. I trusted Him. I had been to other events and retreats, but this was different.

That weekend, I experienced authentic sisterhood. God's heart for women. A kingdom sisterhood. Those sisters partnered with heaven and helped me along my journey to discover all of whom God created me to be.

Pillar Three: I Can Do What He Says I Can Do

That retreat was one of those moments in time that you remember for the rest of your life. It was the end of something and the beginning of something else. I went from trying to become me to learning what being me looked like, smelled like, and sounded like. I had to go back to the beginning. What I learned through facilitated encounters with God is who He created me to be. The authentic me. Before the foundation of the world. I went back to the little girl in the light blue tank top with yellow trim and the white shorts with red trim who was in the middle of the floor wearing her grandmother's wig and knee-high boots without shame, judgment, or fear.

I discovered that I was created to be loud, to be seen. Nothing about me is "normal," and neither are you. Our Father uniquely fashions us for love and purpose. *Being* is a continuous state.

I am so in love with who God created me to be. This journey with Him and the community with which He has blessed me is exceedingly and abundantly above all I could have thought or imagined. (Ephesians 3:20) Every season brings new awareness of my being. When I find myself in new situations, and some of those old feelings try to come up, I get the opportunity to sit with God around it and hear His heart on the situation.

I realize that in surrendering my ideas on how things should be, I get to see God's ideas from His vantage point and experience much greater. We are empowered by heaven and equipped by the power of God to do everything He has called us to do in partnership with Him.

REFLECTION

*What do you remember about yourself
that you were told was "wrong?"*

---

*What are you "doing" that is out of alignment
with who God called you to "be"?*

Ask Holy Spirit to remind you of a specific incident where things shifted for you. Write down the first response.

CHAPTER 7

FREEDOM STRATEGY

G od created us for love. His heart is for us to know this love. One of the biggest things that keeps us from experiencing His love is fear.

> [18] There is no fear in love [dread does not exist], but full-grown (complete, perfect) love [a] turns fear out of doors and expels every trace of terror! For fear [b]brings with it the thought of punishment, and [so] he who is afraid has not reached the full maturity of love [is not yet grown into love's complete perfection]. (1 John 4:18 AMP)

God's heart is for us to experience the freedom found in His love. When we know His love by way of intimate relationship with Him. We trust Him. We trust His word. Even His word about us. When we believe.... nothing shall be impossible to him who believes. (Mark 9:23)

On February 22, 2022 (2/22/22), I had a dream. In the dream, God gave me a prayer strategy to be delivered from some things that He revealed in the dream. He said I would help others use this same strategy to be free.

The Framework for Breaking Covenants with Counterfeits

Julia Winston is one of my mentors by way of a few of her facilitated offerings that I participated in. In her book, "Pray the Kingdom Way," which I highly recommend, she gives a great explanation of what a framework of prayer is and what it is not. She compared a framework to scaffolding when building a building. The scaffold is a temporary and secure place for workers to access greater heights. A scaffold provides safety, position, support, and access. Scaffolding doesn't remain once the building is built. It is there to help build, to bring understanding, and to support the final vision.

I will share the framework I use to break covenants with the counterfeits God reveals in my life. Know and understand that freedom from counterfeits is possible through a relationship with God and revelation from God. This process can only be done in partnership with Him.

Repent | Renounce | Reclaim | Receive

When God shows you that you have come into agreement with something that is not His best nor His original intent for your life, you must repent. What does that mean? That means recognizing that the direction that you are going in is not the direction you want to go in any longer and then agreeing with God. In your prayer time, agree with God about what He says concerning the counterfeit. Align your thinking with His. Then, you renounce the agreement. You boldly declare that you are no longer in agreement with the lie. Next, reclaim your authority. Finally, receive the blessing and walk in the truth of who God created you to be.

This may sound like a lot to you. It may even feel too hard for you to do on your own. It's meant to be. This journey is not meant to be walked alone. That's why partnering with God and asking Him to lead you to the right resources and support system to help you on your journey is essential. Community and mentorship saved my life. There are resources available to help you continue this path of breakthrough. Check out my website, erekathomas.com, for more information.

My prayer is that you use this book as a tool for your own journey to the freedom to BE. That you fully understand and receive the love of your Heavenly Father, Jesus, and Holy Spirit. That you grow in intimacy with Them daily, and that you boldly walk in the confidence of knowing that you are here by design and all of who you BE.

BIBLIOGRAPHY

1. covenant. 2024. In Merriam-Webster.com. Retrieved May 12, 2024, from https://www. merriam-webster.com/dictionary/covenant

2. counterfeit. 2024. In Merriam-Webster.com. Retrieved May 12, 2024, from https://www. merriam-webster.com/dictionary/counterfeit

Resource

3. Winston, Julia M. (2023). *Pray the Kingdom Way: A Framework For How to Connect, Co-Create, & Conquer With God For Success In Business.* Kindle Edition.

Made in the USA
Las Vegas, NV
01 June 2024